THE QUICK GUIDE TO READ PEOPLE'S EMOTIONS:

Discover What People Think By Understanding Their Behavior And Better Your Human Relationships. Analyze And Reveal Emotions, Feelings And Thoughts On Sight

Steve Lowndes & Ian Leil

errors, omissions, or inaccuracies.

TABLE OF CONTENTS

INTRODUCTION:

Why do people succeed in life? What helps them achieve what they want and create long lasting connections with others. It is not education nor experience or knowledge.

None of these factors will help you predict and understand if one person will be successful or not.

Just look around, you can see examples of this every day. At work, at home, in school, in your church or in your neighborhood.

You can see smart, well educated people fail and struggle with their everyday life while others with a more lacking skill set or apparently mediocre attributes succeed.

Why does this happen? And most importantly, how?

The key to understanding what's truly going on lies within the concept of Emotional Intelligence, or in short EQ.

It's not as easy to measure as your IQ and it is most certainly hard to show that you possess such skill on your CV, but its power and effectivity is undeniable.

The existence of emotional intelligence is not some incredible secret, in fact it's been well known for years, what most people truly lack is the ability to understand it and use it.

Many underestimate the power of understanding our own emotions and the emotions of others and do not realize that this is a skill needed to succeed in any field imaginable.

When you are selling something, you need to understand what kind of emotion your approach and your product will create in your spectators.

When you are watching TV or youtube, the content creators are trying to get you to feel certain emotions in order to obtain a positive or negative reaction from you and influence you.

Influencers study emotional intelligence, the most successful marketers study emotional intelligence and the list goes on and on.

Everything that surrounds you revolves around the manipulation and understanding of emotions and since our life is influenced by them so much every day, it is fundamental that we understand how they work to use them at our own advantage.

Most people confuse emotional intelligence with charisma or personality and think that it is not something you can improve. Something that you either have or you don't.

Well, that's not the case and if you pay close attention to what I'm about to tell you, you will understand why.

Don't worry if everything I say doesn't seem immediately clear or it doesn't resonate with you straight away. Absorbing all of this information may take you two or even three readings but I can assure you that it's totally worth it and that this book will completely change the way you think about success.

Without further ado let's dive straight into this emotional intelligence guide!

12

CHAPTER 1:
EMOTIONAL INTELLIGENCE AND THE 4 PILLARS

Dealing effectively with emotions is a daily challenge we all face as our brains are programmed to always let emotions win over our rationality.

Everything you feel, see, hear, smell, touch or taste is goes through your body as an electric signal and its destination is your brain and your frontal lobe, reaching ultimately the place where all of your rational and logical thinking takes place.

There is one important step that has to be noted though: right before reaching your brain, these electric stimuli go through your limbic system.

What does this mean?

Well your limbic system is the place where your emotions are created. This makes it so BEFORE experiencing anything rationally, we experience it emotionally.

These two areas (your frontal lobe and your limbic system) influence each other but your brain cannot stop what your limbic system makes you FEEL emotionally before reason takes over.

This is where emotional intelligence is born, it's the result of the communication between your emotional feelings and your rational thoughts.

Emotional intelligence was a massive discovery as it was the missing link needed to understand why people with the highest IQ would outperform people with average IQ only about 20% of the time.

As you are probably thinking now, this shifted completely the parameters we used to attribute success to.

Emotions can influence you positively or negatively but until you actually understand them you will be just a victim of them, like a tiny boat in a stormy sea.

Without further ado let's dive straight into the 4 big pillars of emotional intelligence that will completely reshape your relationship with emotions!

16

CHAPTER 2:
THE FIRST PILLAR

Self-Awareness.

Self-awareness is the first and most important skill you will need to acquire.

It refers to the ability of absorbing emotional information around you and effectively analyzing it to immediately have a clear view of the situation you find yourself in at that very moment.

As you can imagine, this is a great tool to have at your disposal as it will allow you not only to stay on top of your reactions to different challenges but also to understand your current position in the events developing around you.

Understanding your own tendencies before you start analyzing your surroundings is extremely important. This also means that the more self aware you become, the more in touch you will be with your emotions and your willingness to also focus on negative feelings of discomfort will be a key to your success.

There is no magic shortcut or method when it comes to understanding your emotions, the more time you spend thinking through them and trying to figure out where they come from, the better you will become at reading other people too.

Something that helped me a lot through my journey towards the discovery and understanding of my inner self is the thought that a certain emotion is there for a reason: emotions always have a purpose.

You may think that some of the things that get a negative or positive reaction out of you are random but that's not the case, and it's important for you to understand why such things flick your inner switches.

They are most likely reactions to prior life experiences.

Self awareness' ultimate goal is not to uncover your deepest and dark fears or secrets, its goal is to help you develop a honest understanding of yourself, your skills, what you do well and why, what motivates you, what makes you happy and what kind of situations push your buttons.

Simply thinking about self awareness is the first step towards improving this skill, even if it may seem to you like you are only focusing on what you do wrong, you will overcome the fear of making mistakes and embrace all of your emotions.

It's a fundamental skill and the reason I decided to list it as the first pillar is because the better you become at it, the easier it will be to use the other 3.

Self-awareness is so powerful that a recent study proved that no matter the job (3 different job offices and 3 manual labour jobs were taken into account), about 82% of people high in self-awareness are top performers, and just 3 percent of bottom performers are high in self-awareness.

When you are self aware, you are able to stop your emotions from holding you back and put your efforts into the right direction to achieve your full potential.

CHAPTER 3:
PILLAR ONE MASTERY STRATEGIES

STOP AND THINK

Emotions come and go as they want and you have no power over it. To improve your self awareness, look for the source of your feelings.

Stop and ask yourself why a certain emotion surfaced and made you do something out of character.

As days go by and you are fully absorbed by your routine, hobbies and duties it's really easy to never stop and ask yourself why you did what you just did.

With some practice you can track your reactions back to their origin and understand the purpose of a certain emotional reaction.

These are the questions you should ask yourself.

Why did I react the way I just did?

Can I remember the first time I reacted this way? Who was I with? Who caused this reaction? Is this situation similar to what triggered this emotion for the first time? Does this systematically happen with a specific person?

The biggest challenge to developing self-awareness is objectivity.

Having an objective perspective on your emotions is really tough.

A journal is a great tool to record your thoughts,

emotions and analysis.

You can write down what triggered a certain strong emotion and your reaction and actions following this event.

Write about your day, write about your job, your family, your friends, everything you want.

I can assure you that in just one month your introspection will grow exponentially.

You will start seeing patterns and what emotions and interactions make you feel sad, or happy or get you angry.

Describe your emotions each day but record the physical feelings that show up with your emotions too.

Follow these tricks to start looking within yourself and

developing your self awareness.

Now let's go ahead with the Second Pillar!

26

CHAPTER 4:
THE SECOND PILLAR

Self Management.

Self management is based on your actions, or rather on your ability to take or avoid taking action in a certain situation.

It is your ability to use your newly acquired emotional awareness to manage your reactions in a positive and flexible way.

Some situations might have you paralyzed in terror, making you unable to think clearly and in turn making it impossible to see the possible best course of action.

Self management is your strength in resisting all of the negative internal and external influences you are subject to, when you explore your emotions.

It is not just the ability to hold back and avoid giving in to damaging or problematic behaviour, in fact, bursts of rage or sudden moments of loss of self control, are quite easy to manage and analyze.

What will truly benefit your personal growth is learning to manage your tendencies and habits that manifest themselves on a daily basis, evolving and acquiring new skills to reach bigger goals.

We are talking about a long term investment on yourself. Your goals won't always be immediate and easy to reach, you will have to fight yourself and self manage your inner tendencies over and over again.

True success comes for those individuals who can put every single one of their needs on stand by to focus on what truly matters for them.

CHAPTER 5:
PILLAR TWO MASTERY STRATEGIES

Dedicate some time every day to think through your problems.

We experience countless emotions daily, most of which we are not even aware.

All these feelings create confusing and can influence our choices negatively.

If you think about it, I'm sure you will find that some decisions that you made in a hurry in recent times were not very effective.

The only way to gain some clarity is to dedicate part of your daily schedule to your problems and to reflect on how to solve them efficiently.

We are not talking about hours, just fifteen to twenty minutes will be enough.

Go for a walk or sit at a table, turn off your pc and phone, no music, just be by yourself and meditate.

Your decisions will not be influenced by temporary emotions.

Secondly, sleep on your thoughts.

Jumping to action is not always the best decision, especially if a certain course of actions requires us to be patient.

Before taking a new step ahead, you need to give yourself time to stay in control.

Do not hurry through life, waiting may allow certain factors to surface and help you take your decision.

Time is on your side, it brings clarity and control over your emotions.

Lastly, pay attention to your breath.

And no, I'm not referring to the smell of it, I mean the rhythm of your breaths.

Most people only breath in small short bursts that don't allow their body to get enough oxygen to power their brain and internal organs optimally.

Did you know that the amount of oxygen in your body also influences your mood?

Taking deep breaths using your diaphragm will help you stay focused and alert, so that you can think clearly and effectively while calming your brain.

CHAPTER 6:
THE THIRD PILLAR

Social Awareness.

Social Awareness is a powerful skill: it's the ability of picking up emotional responses and feelings in a person.

It's great and it will allow you to truly understand what is happening around you and what's going on.

You don't have to necessarily feel the same way as someone else to catch how they are feeling, I know it's easy to get lost in our own emotions to the point of forgetting to take into account what someone else is experiencing.

This is when social awareness comes into play to make it so you will still absorb critical information from your surroundings.

It is based off two principles: to listen and to observe.

Stop talking, stop your inner monologue, don't try to predict what someone else is going to say.

This is going to take a lot of practice, I know it did for me, and at times you will feel more like an observer rather than an active participant but it's all for a greater good.

Because you will still be there.

This is not bird watching, you will be a very aware and active part of the events that are unfolding in front of your very eyes.

CHAPTER 7:
PILLAR THREE MASTERY STRATEGIES

Here's a few tricks I want you to practice in order to boost your presence in a room and show people that you pay attention to them, that you are AWARE of yourself and your surroundings.

First of all, simple but quite effective, call and greet everyone by their first name.

Every name has a story behind it and it's a key part of a person's identity.

It really feels great to have someone you just met remember your name and it's going to immediately allow you to gain someone's respect and trust.

This is the most basic yet influential strategy there is to boost your social awareness.

It's going to make any conversation more personable and you will be noticed and remembered more by your interlocutors.

Secondly, pay close attention to body language.

A change in someone's behaviour can tell you loads of things.

Posture, eye movement, expressions and gesture matter a lot and will directly and indirectly communicate with people around you.

By becoming more aware of body language, you will be able to tell how people are
really feeling so that you can act and respond accordingly.

Always start analyzing someone by their head and face, our eyes are extremely talkative, just don't stare for too long.

A good amount of eye contact rather than moving your eyes around all the time, especially as you speak, is going to show that you are a trustworthy person.

Every once in a while look at their mouth too. Are they holding a fake smile? Do they look sad, disappointed, concerned?

Are their shoulders held upright or slouched? Are they standing still or do they keep moving their weight from one leg to the other?

The body is a continuous source of information, pay close attention to it and you will be rewarded.

Thirdly, just stop talking every once in a while and turn into an attentive listener.

When someone speaks to you, stop everything you are doing and listen carefully until they are done.

Don't be on your phone, don't look at your laptop, don't play around with items on your desk.

When you eat dinner with friends or family, turn off the tv and listen.

These tips will help you actually BE THERE and live in the present, paying full attention to the people around you.

43

CHAPTER 8:
THE FOURTH PILLAR

Relationship Management.

Relationship management is the last pillar I will talk about in this book and it will require skills from all previous pillars in order to be acquired.

This is when it all comes together: relationship management is the skill of using your own emotional control and the ability of reading the emotions of other to communicate clearly and effectively and to always be on top of your interactions with other humans, especially during conflict.

You must be able to connect with people over time and to create a bond.

It doesn't matter if you like that person or not, the ultimate benefit is greater than that.

Strong and healthy relationships are something you should always look for, in your private life, at work and even in random places like the gym.

How well you understand people will dictate how well you can connect with them.

Do you want people to listen to you? Then you will have to try and understand them and their needs.

This is a great challenge, especially during tough times

Stressful job environments will be a way to prove yourself and how you can de escalate conflicts by turning such situations into constructive conversations while keeping your anger and personal issues out of it.

47

CHAPTER 9:
PILLAR FOUR MASTERY STRATEGIES

Take well constructive criticism, avoid giving people mixed signals and eventually build trust.

Building relationships is part of any job, even if you work with only one colleague.

You may think that actually MAINTAINING those relationships might not be part of your job but in order to achieve success, you will need to be open-minded and curious.

This means sharing details about yourself to others, you should obviously choose how open you want to be and to what extent you want to share personal information, but remember, the more people know about you, the less you will be subject to misinterpretation.

But that's not it, you must also be interested in what people will share with you in turn.

That's when curiosity comes into play, learn about others and gain their trust.

Show interest in your tone and ask your questions at the right time and in the right place.

Take some time in your day to identify some relationships that might new some patching and work on them!

Good luck, you will soon notice how much of a difference the four pillars of Emotional Intelligence will make in your life.

CONCLUSION

Improving our ability to read your own emotions and the emotions of others is an incredibly serious step we all need to make in order to improve ourselves and to reach our objectives.

Remember, when you are trying to build a skill, you're trying to rewire your brain, create new neural pathways.

This takes a lot of willpower.

Be patient and keep trying. The results will come in no time bringing nothing but positive responses from the people around you.

Improving your technique using the methods I illustrated in this book will do wonders.

Get back in action and let me know how it goes.

Try out these tricks and improve!

52

Best of luck see you in the next book.

ACKNOWLEDGMENTS

The purpose of our books is to make your life better by improving the very fundamental way you learn new things and clear your confusion and bad habits.

We want to thank you for taking action by reading this book and we hope that you keep on using these simple and efficient methods in order to reach your goal. If you found this helpful, we hope that you can spread the word to everyone around you who struggles with the same problems in order to help them.

We also want to thank all of the members of our publishing team for making this possible.

A special thanks goes also to all of the researchers who study this matter every day at the cost of their own sleep to help us improve our life.

Thank you all.

.